CIVIL WAR
HIGHLIGHTS

TRIUMPH
OF THE UNION

1864–1865

TIM COOKE

Smart Apple Media

This edition published in 2013 by

Smart Apple Media, an imprint of Black Rabbit Books

PO Box 3263, Mankato, MN 56002

www.blackrabbitbooks.com

Brown Bear Books Ltd.
Editorial Director: Lindsey Lowe
Managing Editor: Tim Cooke
Children's Publisher: Anne O'Daly
Picture Manager: Sophie Mortimer
Creative Director: Jeni Child

Library of Congress Cataloging-in-Publication Data
Triumph of the Union : 1864-1865 / edited by Tim Cooke.
     pages cm. -- (Civil War Highlights)
 Includes bibliographical references and index.
 Summary: "Chronologically describes the battles and events of
the last 2 years of the US Civil War, including the fall of Atlanta,
Sherman's March, and the surrender of the Confederacy. Includes
a timeline and study features to help readers focus on important
information"--Provided by publisher.
 ISBN 978-1-59920-816-9 (library binding)
1. United States--History--Civil War, 1861-1865--Campaigns--
Juvenile literature. I. Cooke, Tim, 1961-, editor.
 E470.T75 2013
 973.7'3--dc23
                                                    2012001173

Printed in the United States of America at Corporate
Graphics, North Mankato, Minnesota

PO1437
2-2012

9 8 7 6 5 4 3 2 1

Picture Credits

Front Cover: Library of Congress

Contents

Introduction

By the end of 1863, the South was fighting a war of survival. Its economy was devastated and its military strategy in ruins. Southern troops fought on, but they were delaying the inevitable.

By the end of 1863, the course of the Civil War had been largely set. The North had won a decisive strategic victory at Gettysburg in July 1863, bringing an end to the South's second invasion of Northern territory. There would not be a third. For the South, the war had now become a struggle for surival. President Lincoln's Emancipation Proclamation had turned the war into a struggle to overturn slavery. That ensured that the South would get no help from European nations. It also made available a large supply of manpower to the Northern military forces: African Americans.

In the South, over three years of the Northern blockade of all imports and exports had taken a dreadful toll. Food and

The Union advance on Richmond begins with the Battle of the Wilderness in May 1864.

In the Battle of Mobile Bay in August 1864, the Union Navy showed its clear superiority.

other goods were in short supply. Farms were failing because farmers were away at the front. What little industry the South had could not match the output of weapons, ammunitions, or equipment of the North. Meanwhile the Confederate states were reluctant to grant the national government of Jefferson Davis the central powers it needed to carry on the war. For the South, the writing was on the wall.

In this book

Triumph of the Union describes the major engagements of the last two years of the war, as the North gradually tightened its grip on the rebel states. A timeline that runs across the bottom of the pages throughout the book traces the course of the war on the battlefield and other developments in North America and the rest of the world. At the back of the book is a Need to Know feature, which will help you relate specific subjects to your school studies.

Battle of the Wilderness

In March 1864, President Abraham Lincoln recalled
Ulysses S. Grant from the Western theater of the war. He promoted
Grant and put him in charge of all the Union armies.

A drawing by Edwin
Forbes shows the
Union army's VI
Corps fighting in the
dense undergrowth.

Leaving William T. Sherman in charge in the West, Grant
made his headquarters with the Army of the Potomac
(General George G. Meade remained in charge of the army
itself). Grant and Lincoln planned a series of coordinated Union

1861 January–March

CIVIL WAR

JANUARY 2, SOUTH CAROLINA
Fort Johnson in Charleston Harbor is occupied by Confederate troops.

JANUARY 5, ALABAMA Alabama troops seize forts Morgan and Gaines, giving Confederate forces control of Mobile Bay.

JANUARY 9, MISSISSIPPI Leaders vote to leave the Union. Mississippi is the second state to join the Confederacy.

JANUARY 10, FLORIDA Florida leaves the Union.

JANUARY 11, ALABAMA Alabama leaves the Union.

OTHER EVENTS

JANUARY 15, UNITED STATES Engineer Elisha Otis invents the safety elevator.

JANUARY 29, UNITED STATES Kansas joins the Union as the 34th state.

January

campaigns. The Army of the Potomac would advance overland through Virginia toward Richmond, the Confederate capital.

The campaign began on May 3, 1864, when Grant crossed the Rapidan River. He planned to draw Robert E. Lee's Army of Northern Virginia out from its trenches around Richmond. First, however, his 120,000-strong army had to cross the marshes and dense woodland known as the Wilderness. It was the same inhospitable landscape where the Union had been badly defeated a year earlier at the Battle of Chancellorsville.

Union troops moved into the Wilderness on May 4. Although outnumbered, Lee saw that the landscape would take away Grant's advantage. He ordered two corps to advance and ordered another to the front, which would arrive the next day.

Lee takes the initiative

Early on May 5, the Confederates attacked along the Orange Turnpike and the Plank Road. In the thick undergrowth and gunsmoke, the two sides were in places only yards apart and

Alfred Waud's drawing shows Union troops dragging artillery through the mud in March 1864.

JANUARY 19, GEORGIA
Georgia votes to leave the Union.

JANUARY 26, LOUISIANA
Louisiana becomes the sixth state to leave the Union.

FEBRUARY 4, ALABAMA
Leaders from the South meet in the state capital, Montgomery. They choose Jefferson Davis of Mississippi as their president and write a constitution for the Confederate States of America.

FEBRUARY 7, ALABAMA/MISSISSIPPI
The Choctaw Indian Nation forms an alliance with the South. Other Indian tribes follow later.

FEBRUARY, UNITED STATES
The first moving picture system is patented.

MARCH, RUSSIA
Czar Alexander II abolishes serfdom (a form of slavery).

February   March

yet unable to see one another. Exploding shells started fires that raged through the scrub; many of the wounded on both sides burned to death. The battle continued all day in a confusion of noise and smoke, but the Union forces managed to hold on. By the time night fell, Grant and Meade were ready to plan an attack on Lee's right.

James Longstreet, pictured after the war, was seriously injured in the battle.

Longstreet arrives

On May 6, both sides attacked at dawn. By 7:00 A.M. it seemed that Union forces were about to break the Confederate line. Lee's reserve corps, commanded by James Longstreet, had arrived overnight, however. It counterattacked and forced the Union troops to retreat. Using his men's local knowledge, Longstreet used the concealed bed of an unfinished railroad to mount a surprise attack that caught the enemy off guard.

Longstreet's attack could have given the Confederates the chance to drive back the whole of the Union left. In the thick undergrowth, however, they soon lost their momentum. In the chaos, Longstreet's men became muddled with the neighboring corps of A.P. Hill. Longstreet himself was shot in the shoulder by one of his own men. He survived, but would be out of action for several months.

Grant fights back

Grant was determined not to be overawed by Lee's reputation. By late afternoon he had been reinforced by fresh troops and ordered an attack along the Orange Plank Road. Before it

JAMES LONGSTREET

After the war, Longstreet (1821–1904) joined the Republican Party. He became a political ally of his former enemy, President Ulysses S. Grant. That made Longstreet unpopular in the postwar South. Some of his battlefield decisions during the war came to be criticized in retrospect.

1861 April–June

CIVIL WAR

APRIL 12, SOUTH CAROLINA Confederates fire on Fort Sumter in Charleston Harbor in the first shots of the Civil War.

APRIL 15, THE NORTH President Lincoln calls for 75,000 recruits across the North to fight the South.

APRIL 19, WASHINGTON, D.C. President Lincoln declares a naval blockade of Southern states.

APRIL 19, BALTIMORE Mayor George Brown bans Union troops from the city after they are attacked by an angry pro-Confederate mob.

OTHER EVENTS

APRIL, EGYPT A search party sets out from Cairo to find the explorers John Speke and James Grant, who have gone missing while looking for the source of the Nile River.

April

began, however, Lee launched a frontal assault on the Union defenses. The struggle at the Plank Road was ended by the onset of darkness. There was more fighting north of the Orange Turnpike, however. A Confederate attack on the Union right spread panic among troops who remembered the North's painful defeat at Chancellorsville. Again, the arrival of fresh reserves prevented a rout.

Lee had lost 8,700 casualties in the inconclusive battle. Grant's losses were far greater, at 17,000 dead and wounded. Unlike Lee, however, Grant could absorb such losses. Instead of ordering the Army of the Potomac to retreat, as had been the pattern earlier in the war, Grant ordered his troops to advance south toward Spotsylvania in pursuit of the Confederate forces.

Lee would not shake off Grant in Virginia until the day of his surrender at Appomattox in 1865.

This map shows the progress of both sides over the two days of the battle.

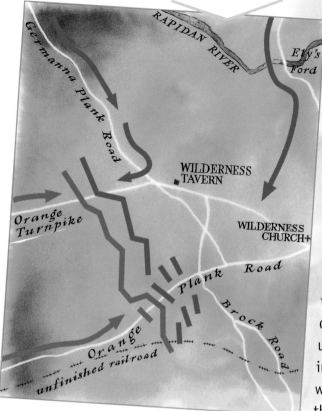

BATTLE DETAILS

1. On May 4 Union troops used the Germanna Plank Road and Ely's Ford to enter the inhospitable Wilderness.

2. On May 5 Lee took the initiative. He sent troops along the Orange Turnpike and the Orange Plank Road. Fighting continued until evening.

3. At dawn on May 6, Union troops were about to break the Confederate line when James Longstreet's reserves counterattacked.

4. Reserves reinforced the Union line later in the day, and fighting went on until dark. The battle ended in a tactical draw, but it was a strategic victory for the Union.

APRIL 23, VIRGINIA Major General Robert E. Lee becomes commander of land and naval forces in Virginia.

APRIL 27, WASHINGTON, D.C. Abraham Lincoln suspends "habeus corpus," a law that protects individuals from being arrested for little reason.

MAY 9, GREAT BRITAIN Britain announces it will remain neutral in the Civil War.

MAY 20, NORTH CAROLINA North Carolina is the last state to leave the Union.

JUNE 20, VIRGINIA West Virginia is unhappy at Virginia's decision to leave the Union. It breaks from the Confederacy and is admitted into the Union.

APRIL, AUSTRALIA Robert Burke and William Wills, who led the first expedition across Australia, narrowly miss their rendezvous with their colleagues; Burke and Wills will die in the Outback.

JUNE, UNITED STATES "Aeronaut" Thaddeus Lowe demonstrates his hot-air balloon for President Abraham Lincoln.

Battle of Spotsylvania

The Battle of Spotsylvania was the second clash of the Union overland campaign in Virginia. Both sides suffered heavy losses—but again, the strategic victory went to the Union.

Some of the most ferocious combat of the whole war took place at the "Bloody Angle," where the Confederate line bulged.

The Battle of the Wilderness (May 5–6, 1864) had had no clear winner. Despite his heavy losses, however, Union commander Ulysses S. Grant was still in a position to advance. He ordered his Army of the Potomac to move south and east

1861
July–September

CIVIL WAR

JULY 2, WISCONSIN Union forces push back Confederates near Hainesville in the Battle of Hoke's Run.

JULY 6, CUBA The Confederate raiding ship CSS *Sumter* captures seven Union vessels in Cuban waters.

JULY 21, VIRGINIA The first major battle of the war is fought at Manassas/First Bull Run. Confederates led by Pierre G.T. Beauregard defeat General Irvin McDowell's larger Union army.

OTHER EVENTS

JULY, UNITED STATES The Pony Express arrives in San Francisco, beginning a cross-country mail service.

JULY, UNITED STATES Congress approves the printing of the first dollar bills, known as "greenbacks."

July

toward Richmond. His initial target was Spotsylvania Courthouse. If he could seize the road junction there, he could cut the Confederate line of supplies.

In fact, Robert E. Lee's Confederates got to Spotsylvania first and set up a defensive line north of the village. The line bulged where it followed some high ground, however, creating a weak point. Union forces attacked the bulge on March 10th and briefly broke the Confederate line. Grant attacked again on the 12th, and again broke through. It was only after desperate hand-to-hand fighting that raged for 24 hours in pouring rain that the Confederates managed to plug the gap.

There were more than 18,000 Union and 12,000 Confederate casualties in the two week battle.

Bitter struggle

The fighting at this point—known as the "Bloody Angle"—was among the most desperate of the war. Flying bullets cut down a tree about 20 inches (50 cm) thick that stood between the lines. Thousands of dead and wounded lay on the earthworks. Confederate counterattacks restored the line. Lee had led a counterattack himself. But by now, he had decided that he needed to move to a stronger position. He withdrew on May 14.

Fighting continued until May 19, when Grant decided to move east to find another route to Richmond. Like the Battle of the Wilderness, Spotsylvania had ended with no clear victory.

AUGUST 10, MISSOURI
The Battle of Wilson's Creek is the first major battle on the Mississippi River; it sees the first death of a Union general, Nathaniel Lyon.

SEPTEMBER 3, KENTUCKY
Confederate forces invade Kentucky, ending its neutrality.

SEPTEMBER 12–15, WEST VIRGINIA
General Robert E. Lee's Confederate forces are beaten at the Battle of Cheat Mountain Summit.

SEPTEMBER 19, KENTUCKY
The Battle of Barbourville sees Confederates raid an empty Union guerrilla training base.

AUGUST, UNITED STATES
The U.S. Government introduces the first income tax to raise funds for the war.

Battle of Cold Harbor

After Wilderness and Spotsylvania, the Union campaign led to central Virginia. The Army of the Potomac and the Army of Northern Virginia clashed at Cold Harbor on June 1 to 3, 1864.

Ulysses S. Grant (leaning over the bench, left) studies a map at the Army headquarters.

It was a month since Ulysses S. Grant had led his Union army into Virginia. In that time, he had fought three battles: at the Wilderness and Spotsylvania, and a smaller clash at North Anna River. Grant had sustained heavy losses, but he had been

1861
October–December

CIVIL WAR

OCTOBER 21, KENTUCKY 7,000 Union troops defeat Confederates at the Battle of Camp Wildcat on Wildcat Mountain.

OCTOBER 21, MISSOURI Union attempts to cross the Potomac River at Harrison's Island fail in the Battle of Ball's Bluff.

OCTOBER 21, MISSOURI The Union controls southeastern Missouri after the Battle of Fredericktown.

NOVEMBER 7, MISSOURI Ulysses S. Grant's Union forces defeat Confederates at the Battle of Belmont.

OTHER EVENTS

OCTOBER 22 UNITED STATES The first telegraph line is completed linking the east and west coasts.

NOVEMBER 1, CONFEDERACY Jefferson Davis is elected as president of the Confederacy.

October

November

unable to strike a decisive blow at Robert E. Lee and the Army of Northern Virginia. Each time, Lee had avoided defeat, and each time he been able to withdraw his troops to keep them between Grant and Richmond, the Confederate capital. Although George G. Meade commanded the Army of the Potomac, the Union campaign was directed by Grant. Richmond remained his ultimate aim. By May 29 the Army of the Potomac was just 11 miles (18 km) northeast of Richmond.

Napoleon 12-pounders were the most widely used Union artillery pieces in the war.

Road to Richmond

Once again, Lee had positioned himself across Grant's line of march. In the east, however, his right flank at Cold Harbor crossroads lay a few miles south of the far left of Grant's line at Bethesda Church. A few miles further south from Cold Harbor lay the Chickahominy River, the last natural obstacle defending Richmond from the Army of the Potomac. If Grant could gain control of the crossroads, the way south to Richmond would again be open. Recognizing the strategic importance of Cold Harbor, both Grant and Lee began to concentrate their armies around it.

First success

On May 31, the battle began with Union success. Philip H. Sheridan led cavalry divisions south to drive off Confederate cavalry holding the Cold Harbor crossroads. Lee sent two

NOVEMBER 8, CUBA
The British steamer *Trent* is stopped by Union warship *San Jacinto* in an action that breaks international law, as Britain is not a combatant in the Civil War.

NOVEMBER 8, KENTUCKY
The Battle of Ivy Mountain, also known as Ivy Creek, sees Union soldiers push Confederates back into Virginia.

DECEMBER 20, VIRGINIA Union troops defeat Confederate cavalry under J.E.B. "Jeb" Stuart in the Battle of Dranesville.

NOVEMBER 19, UNITED STATES
Julia Howe writes the first verses of "The Battle Hymn of the Republic."

DECEMBER 14, GREAT BRITAIN Prince Albert, the husband of Queen Victoria, dies, plunging his wife into a long period of mourning.

An 1864 etching shows Southern women making new uniforms for Confederate troops.

infantry divisions to counterattack, but Meade ordered Sheridan to hold the crossroads "at all hazards." Meade rushed his Union VI Corps to support the cavalry. After a nine-hour overnight march, VI Corps relieved Sheridan's men. They secured the crossroads by 9:00 A.M on June 1.

Grant and Lee arranged their battle lines. By June 2 Cold Harbor lay in the center of a 7-mile (11-km) front that stretched from Bethesda Church to the Chickahominy River. Lee's 58,000 men were the first in position. Grant's five corps—more than 112,000 men—took longer to march on unfamiliar roads in the heat and dust.

Major attack

On June 3, the main Union attack began at 4:30 A.M. From the start, it went wrong. Only three corps at the southern end of the line pressed forward, with disastrous results. The advance met devastating crossfire from dug-in Confederate infantry and artillery. One Union division alone lost more than 1,000 men.

A Union officer later described how "the dreadful storm of lead and iron seemed more like a volcanic blast than a battle." One of his opposing generals was far more blunt in his

EYEWITNESS

"Every corpse I saw was as black as coal.... They were buried where they fell.... I saw no live man lying on this ground. The wounded must have suffered horribly before death relieved them, lying there exposed to the blazing southern sun...."

FRANK WILKESON, AT COLD HARBOR

1862
January–March

CIVIL WAR

JANUARY 18, ARIZONA
The Confederate Territory of Arizona is formed from part of what was the old Territory of New Mexico.

FEBRUARY 6, TENNESSEE
Union General Ulysses S. Grant takes the Confederate Fort Henry. The Tennessee River is now under Union control as far as Alabama.

FEBRUARY 16, TENNESSEE
Grant's troops take Fort Donelson; 15,000 Southerners surrender.

OTHER EVENTS

FEBRUARY, UNITED STATES "The Battle Hymn of the Republic" is published. It quickly becomes a popular marching song in the Union.

January   February

description: he called the fighting murder. The sheer weight of fire had halted the Union advance within a half hour, but Grant did not call off the attack until midday. Both sides dug in along battle lines that they would occupy until June 12.

In his memoirs, Ulysses S. Grant later explained how much he regretted the last attack at Cold Harbor. He wrote, "I have always regretted that the last assault at Cold Harbor was ever made ... No advantage whatever was gained to compensate for the heavy loss we sustained."

Heavy losses

Grant had lost 7,000 casualties for no gain at all. Confederate losses were more like 1,500. Lee had held Grant again, but despite the heavy losses he had inflicted he had not been able to stop the Union advance.

On June 12 Grant withdrew his troops to advance toward the south. This time he crossed the James River to threaten Petersburg and find a new way to Richmond.

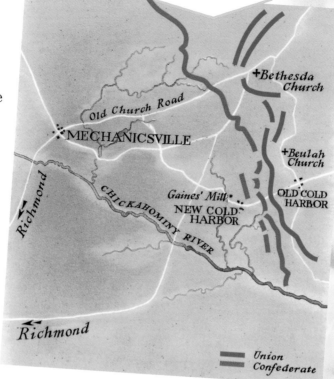

This map details the movements of both sides during the one-sided battle.

BATTLE DETAILS

1. Union cavalry captured Cold Harbor crossroads from Confederate cavalry on May 31. Despite Confederate counterattacks, Union reinforcements secured the crossroads the next day.

2. Over the next 48 hours both armies adjusted their battle lines.

3. Union troops attacked early on June 3, but lost 7,000 troops in just 20 minutes. Grant arrived at midday and called off the assault.

4. The two sides dug in to their lines until June 12, when Grant began to withdraw his men and head south.

FEBRUARY 25, TENNESSEE With the loss of forts Henry and Donelson, Nashville is the first Confederate state capital to fall to Union forces.

MARCH 6–8, ARKANSAS The Confederates are defeated at the Battle of Pea Ridge, the largest battle on Arkansas soil.

MARCH 8–9, VIRGINIA The Battle of Hampton Roads sees Confederate and Union ironclads fight to a standstill.

MARCH 17, VIRGINIA The Union Army of the Potomac sails to Fort Monroe to begin the Peninsular Campaign.

MARCH, EAST AFRICA Zanzibar becomes an independent nation.

MARCH 10, UNITED STATES The first U.S. paper money goes into circulation.

March

Battle of Kennesaw Mountain

While Union troops campaigned in Virginia, General William T. Sherman set out through Georgia. On June 27, 1864, he fought General Joseph E. Johnston at Kennesaw Mountain, near Marietta.

This old photograph shows Kennesaw Mountain in Georgia at about the time of the civil war.

Sherman's march had begun six weeks earlier, on May 5, 1864, when he led nearly 100,000 men—three Union armies—out of Tennessee and south into Georgia. Between him and his destination, Atlanta, lay 60,000 Confederate troops

1862
April–June

CIVIL WAR

APRIL 6–7, TENNESSEE In the Battle of Shiloh Ulysses S. Grant narrowly defeats Confederate forces, with heavy losses on both sides.

APRIL 12, GEORGIA Union agent James Ambrose steals a Confederate train on the Western & Atlantic Railroad. He is captured and hanged.

APRIL 29, THE SOUTH The Confederacy passes a conscription act forcing men aged 18 to 50 to enlist in the army; many farms go into decline as farmers join up.

APRIL 29, LOUISIANA The Union occupation of New Orleans opens access to the rest of Louisiana and the Mississippi Valley.

OTHER EVENTS

APRIL 8 UNITED STATES Inventor John D. Lynde patents the first aerosol spray.

April

commanded by General Joseph E. Johnston. Johnston had taken up a defensive position to invite Sherman to attack. Instead, Sherman tried to maneuver to get around the Confederates. For a month, the armies played cat and mouse. Each time Sherman moved, Johnston moved to block him. Sherman did not want to risk a full attack. As the two forces moved deeper into Georgia, Sherman used his superior numbers to push the enemy back. By mid-June, Johnston occupied a line anchored by Kennesaw Mountain. Sherman believed the Confederate line was stretched. He saw a chance to attack.

A Union disaster

The battle began at dawn on June 27. Sherman sent an advance against Pigeon Hill, south of Kennesaw Mountain. The defenders were well entrenched, however. Their deadly fire forced the attackers to withdraw. The same fate met the main Union attack, a little to the south. Some 8,000 Union troops advanced at a run with their bayonets fixed. They were halted by devastating fire from the Confederate positions. By midday, it was clear that Sherman's men could take no more. The Union had lost more than 3,000 men, dead or wounded; for Johnston, Confederate casualties were just 552.

The disaster convinced Sherman to return to a strategy of maneuver. He raced west for the Chattahoochee River and Atlanta, threatening to outflank Johnston. Johnston also moved south. His only chance to stop Sherman was to find another opportunity to lure his enemy into fighting on ground more favorable to defense.

General Joseph E. Johnston was the highest-ranking U.S. Army officer to resign at the outbreak of war in order to join the Confederate Army.

MAY 31, VIRGINIA
The Battle of Seven Pines is drawn. Union losses are 5,050 and Confederate losses are 6,150.

JUNE 1, VIRGINIA
General Robert E. Lee takes command of the Army of Northern Virgina after General Joseph Johnston is wounded.

JUNE 12, VIRGINIA
J.E.B. Stuart and 1,200 cavalry raid the Union camp outside Richmond, taking 165 prisoners.

JUNE 25, VIRGINIA The first battle of the Seven Days' Campaign— the Battle of Oak Grove—sees McClellan's Union forces halted near Richmond.

MAY 5, MEXICO
A Mexican army defeats an invading French force in the Battle of Puebla.

MAY 20, UNITED STATES
The Homestead Act makes millions of acres of Western land available to settlers.

May   June

Fall of Atlanta

Atlanta had been a Union target since the start of the war.
The so-called Gateway City lay at the heart of the Confederacy. The
four-month struggle for the city in 1864 was a decisive campaign.

A photograph shows the damage done to a house in Atlanta by the Union bombardment.

Atlanta's importance lay in its position as a key railroad
center. It was also an industrial city whose factories
produced many military goods. Atlanta was the South's most
important city after the capital at Richmond, Virginia.

1862
July–September

CIVIL WAR

JULY 1, WASHINGTON, D.C. The Union introduces an Internal Revenue Act, imposing a tax on income to raise money to pay for the war.

JULY 13, WASHINGTON, D.C. President Lincoln reads a draft of the Emancipation Proclamation to his cabinet.

JULY 17, THE NORTH The Confiscation Act and Militia Act come into force, opening the way for the creation of black regiments of freed slaves.

AUGUST 29, VIRGINIA The Second Battle of Bull Run (Manassas) begins.

OTHER EVENTS

JULY 4, GREAT BRITAIN Lewis Carroll makes up the story that will become Alice in Wonderland to amuse a young friend.

JULY 14, UNITED STATES Congress introduces the Medal of Honor for valor in the military services.

July

August

The Union commander ordered to capture Atlanta was General William T. Sherman. On May 7, 1864, he had led his three Union armies south into Georgia from Chattanooga, Tennessee, and Ringgold, Georgia. Facing Sherman was Joseph E. Johnston, one of the most senior Confederate generals. Johnston had only about 60,000 men to face Sherman's 100,000. Johnston had two advantages, however. First, the mountainous terrain favored a side like his that was fighting on the defensive. Second, Sherman's advance into Georgia stretched Union supply lines. Johnston believed that, if he fell back far enough, he would get a chance to counterattack. Sherman, meanwhile, planned to outflank the Confederates.

This photograph shows the ruins of Fort Morgan, Mobile Point, Alabama, after the Union siege.

For two months, neither commander could find a chance to strike at the other. The first major battle of the campaign came on June 27 at Kennesaw Mountain, about 20 miles (32 km) northwest of Atlanta. Believing that Johnston's line was weak, Sherman pushed his men forward and lost 3,000 troops in a series of doomed attacks. Johnston's losses were fewer than 1,000.

Sherman approaches Atlanta

Battered, Sherman resumed his war of maneuver in an attempt to outflank Johnston's army. On July 8 he finally managed to cross the Chattahoochee River. Atlanta lay only 7 miles (11 km) away, with no more natural barriers to protect it. Johnston's army remained undefeated, but the enemy was now on the edge of victory and Johnston would pay the price.

AUGUST 30, VIRGINIA
Confederate Robert E. Lee defeats the Union army at Bull Run. His casualties stand at 9,500, while Union losses are 14,500.

SEPTEMBER 17, MARYLAND
The Battle of Antietam ends in a draw after heavy losses on both sides: Lee's Army of Northern Virginia suffers 10,000 casualties; the Union Army of the Potomac loses 12,400 dead, wounded, or missing.

SEPTEMBER 22, WASHINGTON, D.C.
Lincoln issues a preliminary Emancipation Proclamation.

SEPTEMBER 24, TENNESSEE
Union General William Sherman orders the destruction of every house in Randolph in revenge for Confederate shelling of his steamboats.

AUGUST 18, UNITED STATES An uprising by young Sioux Indians in Minnesota leaves more than 800 white settlers dead.

September

This photograph shows a railroad destroyed by Hood's Confederate troops.

Confederate President Jefferson Davis believed that Johnston's strategy had been unacceptably passive. On July 17 he replaced Johnston as commander of the Army of Tennessee. The new commander was General John Bell Hood, who had a reputation for fighting spirit and aggression that sometimes verged on recklessness.

Hood defends Atlanta

Under Johnston, the campaign had been based largely on maneuver; under Hood, it became a series of headlong battles. On July 20, Hood attacked part of Sherman's army at Peachtree Creek. He lost nearly 5,000 men compared with fewer than 2,000 Union casualties. Two days later he lost another 8,000 men when he attacked in the Battle of Atlanta. After two rapid defeats, Hood pulled his army back to defensive positions surrounding Atlanta.

Sherman could see that the fortifications were too strong for a direct assault. Instead, he bombarded the city while he sent his troops to cut the supply lines that linked Atlanta to the rest of the South. In August the Macon and Western Railroad became the focus of a struggle for control. The struggle ended on August 31 and September 1, when the Confederates lost two battles at Jonesboro, 15 miles (24 km) south of Atlanta. Having lost control of the railroad, Hood abandoned Atlanta.

A DISASTROUS LEADER

John Bell Hood (1831–1879) rose quickly through Confederate ranks. While he was an effective and aggressive division commander, he was a disaster as commander of the Army of Tennessee. He led his troops nearly to destruction.

1862
October–December

CIVIL WAR

OCTOBER 3, MISSISSIPPI
A Union army defeats the Confederates in the Battle of Corinth.

OCTOBER 11, VIRGINIA
The Confederate Congress passes an unpopular draft law that exempts anyone owning more than 20 slaves—the wealthiest part of society—from military service.

NOVEMBER 7, WASHINGTON, D.C.
Lincoln fires George B. McClellan as commander of the Army of the Potomac and appoints Ambrose E. Burnside in his place.

OTHER EVENTS

OCTOBER 8, PRUSSIA Otto von Bismarck becomes minister-president of Prussia; he uses his position to mastermind the unification of Germany.

NOVEMBER 4, UNITED STATES
Richard Gatling patents the machine gunthat is named for him: the Gatling gun.

October   November

On September 2, Union forces marched into the city. The campaign had cost the Union 5,000 dead, 25,000 wounded, and 5,000 missing: a total of 35,000. The cost of the failed Confederate defense was virtually identical: 35,200.

A boost for Lincoln

For President Abraham Lincoln, the fall of Atlanta came just at the right time. Only a month earlier, he had been worried that he would lose the presidential elections due in November. A summer of military stalemate had crushed morale in the North. But the fall of Atlanta clearly showed that the Union was winning the war.

The news electrified the North. It also stimulated renewed support for Lincoln. The fall of Atlanta was probably the biggest single factor behind Lincoln's victory in the 1864 election. For the South, the defeat was crushing. It had lost a rail and manufacturing center. The Deep South lay open to further Union offensives.

The depots and factories of Atlanta, Georgia, are set on fire by Union troops.

PROTECTING THE RAILROADS

Railroads captured by Union forces in the South became targets in turn for raids by Confederate cavalry. Raiders such as Nathan Bedford Forrest and John Hunt Morgan could move around easily, tearing up tracks, burning bridges, and destroying or stealing supplies. This forced the Union to protect the railroads with blockhouses garrisoned by hundreds of troops. One such blockhouse, attacked by Forrest near Athens, Alabama, in 1864 resembled a small fort. The Confederates sometimes used artillery to destroy the blockhouses. The fight for the railroads was a war of its own.

DECEMBER 7, TENNESSEE
Confederates defeat Union troops at the Battle of Hartsville, opening parts of western Tennessee and Kentucky.

DECEMBER 13–14, VIRGINIA
Burnside is beaten back in the Battle of Fredericksburg, with the loss of 6,500 Union troops.

DECEMBER 31, TENNESSEE
Union troops triumph in the Battle of Murfreesboro, taking Kentucky and increasing their hold on Tennessee.

DECEMBER 30, UNITED STATES
Lincoln reads his Emancipation Proclamation to his cabinet for comments.

DECEMBER 31, UNITED STATES
Lincoln signs an act admitting West Virginia to the Union.

Battle of Jonesboro

By the end of July 1864, Union General William T. Sherman was outside Atlanta, Georgia. The city was defended by John Bell Hood's Confederate Army of Tennessee.

Union forces attack the outnumbered Confederates at Jonesboro on September 1, 1864.

Sherman had outflanked the Army of Tennessee on his campaign through Georgia. The Confederate commander, Joseph E. Johnston, had been fired and replaced by John Bell Hood, who retreated into Atlanta. Sherman began an artillery

1863 January–March

CIVIL WAR

JANUARY 1, WASHINGTON, D.C.
The Emancipation Proclamation comes into effect, ruling that slaves in the South are free. The Civil War is now a war for the abolition of slavery, as well as a struggle to preserve the Union.

JANUARY 20–22, VIRGINIA
The Union Army of the Potomac tries to cross the Rappahannock River but turns back as rain turns the ground to mud.

OTHER EVENTS

JANUARY 1, UNITED STATES
The Homestead Act comes into law, encouraging western migration by granting land to farmers.

JANUARY 10, GREAT BRITAIN
The world's first underground railroad line opens in London.

FEBRUARY 3, UNITED STATES
Newspaper editor Samuel Clemens first uses the pen name by which he will become famous: Mark Twain.

January

February

bombardment of the city, but realized that it was too well defended for a direct assault.

On August 25 Sherman sent his forces south and west to cut Atlanta's railroad links. Hood, who had a reputation for being reckless, believed Sherman was retreating. When enemy troops were spotted south of Atlanta, at Jonesboro, he sent William J. Hardee to deal with what he assumed was a raiding party.

In fact, on August 31 the astonished Hardee blundered into almost the whole of Sherman's army. The Confederates tried an attack, but suffered high casualties for no gain. This failure forced another Confederate corps to fall back to the Macon and Western Railroad. On September 1 Sherman drove off the Confederate defenders and cut the railroad north of Jonesboro. Atlanta's last supply line was cut. Hood had no choice but to evacuate the city. The Conferates left on the night of September 1; Sherman's men entered the city the next day.

The capture of the city had cost 1,150 casualties, making a total of 35,000 for Sherman's Atlanta campaign. For Abraham Lincoln, however, the victory was welcome. It boosted his popularity as presidential elections approached. Any lingering hopes that the Confederacy might defeat the North had now gone. The loss of Atlanta sealed the defeat of the South.

Union General William T. Sherman captured Atlanta on September 2, 1864, after a four-month campaign.

MARCH 3, WASHINGTON, D.C.
The Union introduces the National Conscription Act, obliging men to join the army or pay $300 to hire a substitute.

MARCH 3, THE SOUTH
The Confederacy introduces an unpopular Impressment Act that allows army officers to take food from farmers at set rates.

FEBRUARY 24, UNITED STATES
Arizona is organized as a territory of the United States.

MARCH 3, UNITED STATES
The territory of Idaho is created.

March

Battle of Mobile Bay

The naval battle that was fought for control of Mobile Bay, Alabama, on August 5, 1864, became famous for a legendary order given by Union admiral David G. Farragut.

Even though it is outnumbered, the Confederate ironclad CSS *Tennessee* (center) fights on.

The capture of Mobile Bay was the final step in the Union campaign to stop Confederate efforts breaking the Union's blockade of the South's sea trade. The bay was used by blockade runners, ships that used their speed to outrun the Union vessels

1863
April–June

CIVIL WAR

APRIL 2, VIRGINIA "Bread riots" break out in the Confederacy over the high price of food; the worst riots are in Richmond.

APRIL 17, MISSISSIPPI Union cavalry raids Mississippi, tearing up railroad lines. Soldiers ride south to the Union city of Baton Rouge, Louisiana.

MAY 2–4, VIRGINIA The Confederate Army of Northern Virginia defeats the Union Army of the Potomac at the Battle of Chancellorsville; however, Confederate commander "Stonewall" Jackson is shot by one of his own men and dies.

MAY 14, MISSISSIPPI Union troops capture Jackson, the fourth state capital to fall to Union troops.

OTHER EVENTS

MAY 22, UNITED STATES The War Department establishes the Bureau of Colored Troops.

April

May

trying to stop them. On August 5, 1864, David G. Farragut sailed into the bay with a Union fleet of 14 wooden ships, 4 ironclad monitors, 2,700 men, and 197 guns.

The bay was well defended. At its entrance stood forts Morgan and Gaines. The entrance was also blocked by sea mines (known as torpedoes). Facing Farragut under Franklin Buchanan were the ironclad CSS *Tennessee*, 3 wooden ships, 427 men, and 22 guns.

Union sailors pose on deck with a battery of 11-inch (28-cm) Dahlgren guns on the USS *Pawnee*.

Rallying cry

The Union vessels opened fire, but the ironclad USS *Tecumseh* hit a mine and sank. The captain of the USS *Brooklyn* hesitated and signaled Farragut for advice. From his flagship, Farragut issued what became one of the most famous orders of the whole war: "Damn the torpedoes! Full speed ahead!"

From his flagship, USS *Hartford*, Farragut led the rest of the Union fleet into the bay. The wooden Confederate ships were soon overwhelmed, but the *Tennessee* fought on alone for almost two hours. Again and again, Union ships rammed it at full speed until, badly damaged, it surrendered.

The battle had lasted three hours, and each side had suffered 300 casualties. The Confederates would keep control of the city of Mobile for eight months, but Farragut had closed the port—and struck another blow at the Southern economy.

MAY 18, MISSISSIPPI
Union armies begin the siege of Vicksburg.

JUNE 9, VIRGINIA
The Battle of Brandy Station ends in a Confederate victory.

JUNE 14, VIRGINIA
The Battle of Winchester is another Confederate victory.

JUNE 16, VIRGINIA
Lee orders the Army of Northern Virginia across the Potomac River to invade the North for a second time.

JUNE 28, WASHINGTON, D.C.
Lincoln replaces General Joseph Hooker as commander of the Army of the Potomac with General George Meade, whom he hopes will be more aggressive.

JUNE 7, MEXICO French troops capture Mexico City; the French want to begin a colony while Americans are distracted by the war.

JUNE 20, UNITED STATES
West Virginia is admitted to the Union following a presidential proclamation.

Siege of Petersburg

Petersburg, Virginia, was a key railroad center. Having trapped
Robert E. Lee there, Union General Ulysses S. Grant besieged the
city for 10 months from June 1864.

Union soldiers pose
at a heavily
reinforced dugout,
or bombproof,
during the siege.

Lee was forced to order much of his army to defend
Petersburg's strategic location after a rapid advance by the
Union Army of the Potomac. Grant had sent 100,000 men of the
Army of the Potomac south from Cold Harbor. He intended them

1863
July–September

CIVIL WAR

**JULY 1–3,
PENNSYLVANIA**
The Battle of Gettysburg
yields 20,000 casualties
on each side in a
decisive Union victory
that marks a turning
point in the war.

JULY 4, MISSISSIPPI
The fall of Vicksburg
to the Union splits the
Confederacy in two.

JULY 13, NEW YORK
Antidraft riots erupt
across the North; in the
worst, in New York City,
African Americans are
attacked and draft
offices burned.

**JULY 18,
SOUTH CAROLINA**
The 54th Massachusetts
Volunteer Infantry, a
black Union unit, fails
in a courageous attack
on Fort Wagner.

OTHER EVENTS

JULY 1, SOUTH AMERICA
The Dutch abolish slavery
in their colony of Suriname.

JULY, CAMBODIA French writers
reveal for the first time the existence
of the remarkable ruined city of
Angkor in the Cambodian jungle.

July

to cross the James River, swing west through Petersburg, and attack Lee from the rear. Only a Confederate force hastily gathered by General Pierre G.T. Beauregard halted the Union advance at Petersburg.

Lee headed south to reinforce the city. His forces set up lines of fortifications southeast of the city, facing the route of the Union advance. Instead, Grant's attacks came from the west and south. Their targets were the two railroads that kept Lee supplied in Petersburg, and the Appomattox River, which marked Lee's line of retreat to the west.

Confederate ordeal

Grant laid siege to the city. In late August Union forces cut the railroad running south. More attacks in late September and late October strengthened the Union trenches around the city and threatened the last open rail line. Heavily outnumbered, Lee faced a desperate winter of trench warfare. He did not even have enough troops to man all the fortifications.

In spring 1865, Grant renewed his attacks. On March 29, he sent 125,000 men to outflank Lee's trenches. On April 1 the Union force pushed aside just 10,000 Confederates at the Battle of Five Forks. With his line of retreat threatened, Lee evacuated Petersburg on April 2. It was the beginning of the end for his army.

Union troops crowd into the trenches during the Siege of Petersburg.

AUGUST 17, SOUTH CAROLINA Union forces begin a bombardment of Fort Sumter in Charleston Harbor, the place where the first shots of the war were fired.

AUGUST 20, KANSAS William Quantrill's Confederate guerrillas attack Lawrence, killing more than 150 civilians and destroying 200 buildings.

SEPTEMBER 19–20, TENNESSEE Confederates win a hollow victory at the two-day Battle of Chickamauga, losing 18,000 to the Union's 16,000, and forcing only a partial Union withdrawal to Chattanooga.

SEPTEMBER 29, ITALY Troops led by the nationalist Giuseppe Garibaldi defeat a papal army, a major obstruction to Italian unification.

Sherman's March

In late 1864 Union General William T. Sherman marched through the South. He left such destruction behind that many Southerners saw his campaign as little more than a war crime.

The 21st Michigan Infantry were with Sherman on his March to the Sea in 1864.

Sherman's march had two purposes. The first was practical, and the second was psychological. In practical terms, Sherman wanted to establish a secure source of supplies for his army. After capturing Atlanta, Georgia, on September 2, 1864,

1863
October–December

CIVIL WAR

OCTOBER 15, SOUTH CAROLINA
Confederate submarine *H.L. Hunley* sinks on its second test voyage, drowning all its crew.

NOVEMBER 19, PENNSYLVANIA
Lincoln makes his famous "Gettysburg Address" during the dedication of the cemetery on the battlefield.

OTHER EVENTS

OCTOBER 3, UNITED STATES
President Abraham Lincoln proclaims the last Thursday in November as Thanksgiving Day.

OCTOBER 23, SWITZERLAND
The first conference of the International Committee of the Red Cross is held.

NOVEMBER 23, UNITED STATES
A patent is granted to the first process for color photography.

October

November

he allowed his men to rest. But the Confederate Army of the Tennessee constantly threatened to cut his supply line, the railroad from Chattanooga, Tennessee. Deciding that it was impossible to protect the entire length of the railroad, Sherman proposed to march to the port of Savannah, Georgia, on the Atlantic Coast 220 miles (352 km) away. If he captured the port, he could use Union ships to supply his army.

Sherman also saw the march as a chance to strike a psychological blow to the Confederacy. He believed in "total war." He could break Southern resistance by making civilians suffer, as well as the military. On their march, his troops would cut supply lines and "smash things generally." The Union army would live off the land, taking what it wanted from Georgia farms.

In November 1864, Sherman sent 35,000 troops back to defend Nashville from attempts to invade Union-occupied Tennessee. Then he burned everything of Atlanta that had any military use. On November 15 he set out southeast with 60,000 men on his "March to the Sea" to Savannah.

Scenes depicting events from Sherman's March to the Sea through Georgia, published in *Harper's Weekly*.

March of destruction

As Sherman had predicted, the Confederate Army of Tennessee did indeed launch an invasion of Tennessee. Not only did it fail badly, but it also left no forces to oppose Sherman's march except some Confederate cavalry and Georgia militia. That

NOVEMBER 23, TENNESSEE
The Battle of Chattanooga sees Union troops push back the Confederates.

NOVEMBER 24–25, TENNESSEE The Union capture of Chattanooga opens the "Gateway to the South."

DECEMBER 1, WASHINGTON, D.C.
Confederate spy Belle Boyd is freed from prison by Union authorities.

DECEMBER 9, TENNESSEE
After a 16-day siege, Confederate defenders withdraw from the town of Knoxville.

DECEMBER 16, TENNESSEE General Joseph Johnston takes command of the Confederate Army of Tennessee, replacing General William Hardee.

NOVEMBER 26, UNITED STATES
The first modern Thanksgiving Day is celebrated in the North.

DECEMBER 1, CHILE
A fire in a church causes panic in which 1,500 worshipers die.

SHERMAN'S NECKTIES

Sherman's troops destroyed everything they came across, including railroads. Their favored technique was to heat the rails over fires and twist them around trees. These "Sherman's neckties" became a common sight along the route of the march.

made Sherman's job of supplying his army much easier. He was able to spread his army in a dispersed line 60 miles (96 km) wide. Each day parties of men set out to forage for supplies, like fresh meat, corn, and other foods.

As the Union troops advanced, they pulled up railroads and set fire to factories. Anything that might be valuable to the Confederate war effort was a legitimate target. But there were also many cases of unauthorized theft and vandalism. The thousands of stragglers who followed the army were lawless and beyond military control. Even battle-hardened veterans were unhappy about how harshly civilians were treated. Some of those who were treated worse were African American slaves. The Union army liberated them—but then wanted nothing to do with them.

On December 21, 1864, Sherman occupied Savannah. He then prepared to join forces with Ulysses S. Grant in Virginia to defeat Robert E. Lee's army. Sherman thought about moving his troops to Virginia by sea. Instead, he decided to continue his strategy with a second march through the Carolinas.

Confederates defend Fort Fisher, North Carolina, the last major Southern stronghold.

Through the Carolinas

The Carolinas march began on February 1, 1865. It was more challenging than the first. There were more Confederate troops in the way, and Sherman's route lay along muddy roads and across swampy rivers. Still, Confederate commanders were surprised by

1864 January–March

CIVIL WAR

JANUARY 14, GEORGIA Union General William T. Sherman begins his infamous March through the South.

JANUARY 17, TENNESSEE At the Battle of Dandridge, Confederate forces repel Union troops from the Dandridge area.

FEBRUARY 9, VIRGINIA A total of 109 Union prisoners escape through a tunnel at Libby Prison in Richmond.

FEBRUARY 14–20, MISSISSIPPI In the Battle of Meridian, William T. Sherman leads a successful Union raid to destroy an important railroad junction.

OTHER EVENTS

FEBRUARY 1, DENMARK Prussian forces invade the Danish province of Schleswig, beginning the Second Schleswig War.

January   February

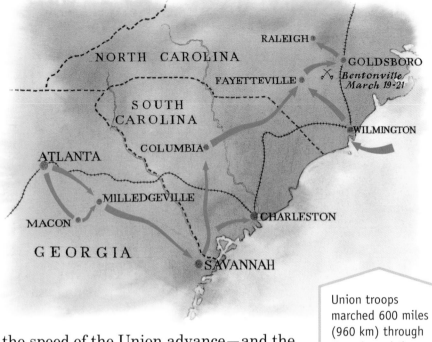

Union troops marched 600 miles (960 km) through Georgia and the Carolinas.

A MUCH-HATED MAN

Sherman's destructive marches made him a figure of hate among Southerners. His troops set out to destroy their homes and way of life. Some slaves welcomed him as their liberator and left their plantations to join him; estimates suggest as many as 10,000 followed the Union troops. But other slaves remained loyal to their owners; they saw Sherman's ransacking of the South as a betrayal. For Sherman, the case was clear: "We are not only fighting armies, but a hostile people, and must make old and young, rich and poor, feel the hard hand of war, as well as their organized armies. I know that this recent movement of mine through Georgia has had a wonderful effect...."

the speed of the Union advance—and the level of ruthlessness they witnessed.

South Carolina suffered far greater destruction than Georgia had. Even towns and homes with no military value were robbed and burned. On February 17–18, 1865, the state capital, Columbia, was destroyed by fire. The event became notorious, but in fact it remains unclear whether Union troops started the blaze intentionally.

There was one last Confederate attempt to stop Sherman, in North Carolina. Joseph E. Johnston had been restored to command and, on March 19–21, he fought Sherman at Bentonville. Victorious, Sherman occupied Raleigh, the state capital. Within weeks the war was over. Johnston surrendered to Sherman on April 26. Sherman's marches had been decisive.

FEBRUARY 20, FLORIDA
Many men of the 8th Regiment of United States Colored Troops are killed or injured in the Battle of Olustee near Jacksonville; Union forces retreat to the coast.

MARCH 2, THE NORTH
Lieutenant General Ulysees S. Grant is made commander of all the armies of the United States.

MARCH 25, KENTUCKY Confederate cavalry attack the city of Paducah on the Ohio River; they retreat the next day, having suffered many casualties.

MARCH 14, AFRICA British explorers Samuel and Florence Baker discover Lake Albert at the headwaters of the Nile River.

Battle of Nashville

As Sherman set out on his "March to the Sea," the Confederates tried to recapture Tennessee. This final Confederate offensive in the West culminated at the Battle of Nashville.

Confederate troops under General Hood camped around Nashville in December 1864.

Sherman's move had given Confederate John Bell Hood a chance to strike back at the Union. If he could recapture Tennessee, Hood would also put pressure on Sherman to abandon his march and turn to deal with the threat.

1864 April–June

CIVIL WAR

APRIL 12, TENNESSEE Confederate troops massacre the Union garrison at Fort Pillow, killing 202 African Americans.

APRIL 17, GEORGIA Hungry citizens of Savannah stage bread riots over the lack of food.

MAY 3, VIRGINIA The Union Army of the Potomac starts to move south, crossing the difficult terrain of the Wilderness region.

OTHER EVENTS

APRIL 10, MEXICO The French proclaim Archduke Maximilian of Austria as emperor of Mexico.

APRIL 22, UNITED STATES Congress decides to print the phrase "In God We Trust" on U.S. coins.

MAY 9, NORTH SEA Austria and Denmark fight a naval battle at Heligoland during the Second Schleswig War.

April   May

In late November, Hood led 30,000 men of the Army of Tennessee north out of Alabama. On 30 November, he defeated a Union force outside Franklin, Tennessee. Despite losing more than 6,200 casualties, Hood kept advancing. The Confederates reached Nashville on December 2. The city was ringed by strong Union fortifications. Hood ordered his men to dig in for a siege.

Disaster for the South

Ulysses S. Grant, the Union supreme commander, did not want to endure a winter siege. He ordered George H. Thomas, commander of the Army of the Cumberland inside Nashville, to attack Hood. After a delay while he prepared his offensive, Thomas attacked early on December 15. Before daylight, a Union attack struck Hood's right flank. At noon, an attack by 35,000 men on Hood's left forced the Confederate back a mile to a strong position protected by Peach Tree Hill on the right and Shy's Hill on the left.

The next day, Thomas attacked again, despite pouring rain and sleet. The Confederate right held, but on the left Shy's Hill fell to the attackers. Union cavalry got around behind the Confederate line. A final attack on the center broke Hood's line.

The Army of Tennessee was routed. Now numbering barely 17,000, it retreated to Tupelo, Mississippi. In January, Hood resigned. In contrast, Thomas was promoted to major general and received the thanks of a grateful U.S. Congress.

The railroad yard in Nashville, Tennessee, photographed in December 1864.

MAY 5–6, VIRGINIA
Grant and Lee fight the inconclusive Battle of the Wilderness.

MAY 12, VIRGINIA
Grant and Lee fight again at the Battle of Spotsylvania. The battle is drawn.

JUNE 3, VIRGINIA
The Battle of Cold Harbor is a disaster for the Union army. They lose 7,000 men for no gain against Confederate losses of 1,500.

JUNE 27, GEORGIA
The Battle of Kennesaw Mountain sees Sherman's Union troops suffer heavy losses of 3,000 against Johnston's Confederate losses of 552.

MAY, GREAT BRITAIN
Charles Dickens publishes the first part of *Our Mutual Friend*.

MAY 26, UNITED STATES
Congress creates the territory of Montana, with its original capital at Virginia City.

JUNE 15, UNITED STATES Secretary of War Edwin M. Stanton creates Arlington National Cemetery, Virginia, on land previously owned by Confederate General Robert E. Lee.

Battle of Five Forks

Fought on April 1, 1865, the Battle of Five Forks was a decisive engagement in the long siege of Petersburg, Virginia. Defeat made it almost impossible for the Confederates to remain in the city.

At Five Forks the Confederates were routed by General Philip H. Sheridan's Union troops.

Union commander Ulysses S. Grant had besieged his adversary Robert E. Lee inside Petersburg through the winter. Grant had the advantage: Lee was heavily outnumbered and Union forces threatened the railroads that supplied the city.

1864
July–September

CIVIL WAR

JULY 9, MARYLAND Confederates defeat Union troops at the Battle of Monocacy.

JULY 11, WASHINGTON, D.C. Facing strong Union defenses, Confederates withdraw from their attack on the Union capital.

JULY 22, GEORGIA Confederate General Hood's troops fail to defeat General Sherman's men at the Battle of Atlanta. Confederate losses are 8,000; Union losses are 3,600.

AUGUST 5, ALABAMA Union warships defeat Confederate vessels at the Battle of Mobile Bay. Union admiral David G. Farragut is said to have ordered, "Damn the torpedoes; full speed ahead!"

OTHER EVENTS

JULY 5, UNITED STATES The Bank of California is founded with holdings of $2 million.

JULY 14, UNITED STATES Gold is discovered in Montana at Helena, which will later become the state capital.

AUGUST 8, SWITZERLAND The first Geneva Convention is held to discuss the treatment of wounded soldiers in war.

July   August

As spring approached in late March 1865, however, and the muddy roads dried and hardened, Grant feared that Lee might try to evacuate the city. If he escaped westward, he could join a Confederate army in North Carolina. Grant set out to cut Lee's remaining escape routes.

On March 31 elements of the two armies clashed at Dinwiddie, west of Petersburg. Lee ordered the Confederate commander, George E. Pickett, to withdraw to Five Forks. Five roads radiated out from the hamlet, including one that led directly north to Lee's last remaining supply line, the Southside Railroad. Ordered to hold Five Forks, Pickett began building fortifications to shelter his small force of infantry and cavalry.

Interrupted picnic

Union commander Philip H. Sheridan renewed the assault the next day, April 1. At 4:00 P.M. his men charged out of the pine thickets into the Confederate line. Thousands of the defenders were killed and captured; the rest broke and retreated. Pickett was not even present: he was eating a picnic meal with some of his fellow generals. The first he learned of the defeat was when survivors began streaming past. Pickett had no choice but to join the retreat.

The disastrous defeat at Five Forks alone did not cause the fall of Petersburg. When news reached Lee, however, he began preparations to evacuate the city. On April 2 a final Union attack overcame the Petersburg defenses as the Army of Northern Virginia headed west. Its fate was sealed.

This engraving shows the scene at Lincoln's second inauguration on March 4, 1865.

AUGUST 31, ILLINOIS The Democratic National Convention in Chicago nominates General George B. McClellan as its presidential candidate on an antiwar ticket.

SEPTEMBER 1, GEORGIA General Sherman cuts the last supply line to Atlanta, the railroad, forcing the Confederates to leave the city.

SEPTEMBER 16, VIRGINIA Confederate cavalrymen raid Union beef supplies on the James River to feed hungry Southerners.

SEPTEMBER 22, VIRGINIA Union forces defeat Confederates at the Battle of Fisher's Hill and start to destroy crops in the Shenandoah Valley.

SEPTEMBER 5, JAPAN British, Dutch, and French fleets attack Japan to open the Shimonoseki Straits to navigation.

SEPTEMBER 15, ITALY The new country gives up its claims to Rome; the Italians agree to make Florence their capital.

Appomattox Campaign

By spring 1865, the Confederate situation was desperate. The Union was in complete control in the Eastern theater of the war. The Army of Northern Virginia was facing its final defeat.

Union cannon fire on Confederate positions at the siege of Petersburg near the war's end.

The Confederate forces were under pressure on two fronts. In the Carolinas, Joseph E. Johnston's Army of Tennessee faced Union General William T. Sherman. Sherman's marches through Georgia and the Carolinas had captured Charleston

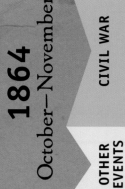

1864
October–November

CIVIL WAR

OCTOBER 19, VIRGINIA
Union forces, under General Sheridan, defeat General Early's Confederate Army of the Valley at the Battle of Cedar Creek.

OCTOBER 26, ALABAMA
Union forces at Decatur prevent Confederates led by John Bell Hood from crossing the Tennessee River in an attempt to cut William T. Sherman's lines of communication.

OCTOBER 27, VIRGINIA
Union forces assaulting the Confederate capital at Richmond are defeated in the Second Battle of Fair Oaks.

OTHER EVENTS

OCTOBER 11, UNITED STATES
Slavery is abolished in Maryland.

OCTOBER 30, AUSTRIA The Peace of Vienna ends the Second Schleswig War between Germany and Denmark.

OCTOBER 31, UNITED STATES
Nevada is admitted to the Union as the 36th state.

October

Union
Confederate

RICHMOND

APPOMATTOX RIVER

Richmond and Danville Railroad

FARMVILLE

SAYLER'S CREEK

APPOMATTOX COURT HOUSE

to Lynchburg

AMELIA COURT HOUSE

JETERSVILLE

BURKEVILLE

PETERSBURG

Southside Railroad

FIVE FORKS
April 1

This map shows the final movements of both sides in the last days of war.

and the last open Confederate port, Wilmington. The campaign had left Johnston's force with just 15,000 infantry and a few thousand cavalry facing almost 90,000 in Sherman's army.

In Virginia, meanwhile, the siege of Petersburg that had begun in June 1864 finally came to an end. Union forces under Ulysses S. Grant defeated the Army of Northern Virginia at Five Forks outside Petersburg on April 1. When they attacked the city's defenses the next day, the Confederates began to retreat from Petersburg. Over the next couple of days, they also abandoned their capital at Richmond.

Facing imminent defeat, Lee planned to move his army west rapidly in order to outpace the Union troops. If he could meet up with Johnston at Danville, they could make a combined stand. But Lee's men were weakened and hungry. He lost a day waiting at Amelia Court House on the Richmond and Danville Railroad for supplies that never arrived. His soldiers searched in vain for food in the surrounding countryside.

NOVEMBER 4, TENNESSEE
Confederate cavalry commander Nathan B. Forrest completes a 23-day raid in Georgia and Tennessee by destroying a Union supply base at Johsonville.

NOVEMBER 15, GEORGIA
Union general William T. Sherman burns much of Atlanta before setting out on his notorious "March to the Sea."

NOVEMBER 25, NEW YORK
Confederate spies fail in a plot to burn down New York City.

NOVEMBER 8, UNITED STATES
Abraham Lincoln is reelected for a second term as president of the United States.

NOVEMBER 29, UNITED STATES
Militia in Colorado massacre some 200 Cheyenne and Arapaho at Sand Creek in retaliation for an attack on settlers.

This photograph shows McLean's house at Appomattox, where Lee surrendered.

On April 5 Union cavalry and infantry skirmished with the Confederates around Amelia Court House and Tabernacle Creek. Meanwhile, Lee had lost his opportunity. Philip H. Sheridan's Union cavalry had outpaced him and blocked the route south at Jetersville on the Richmond and Danville Railroad. Abandoning his original plan, Lee was forced to set out west for Farmville. He ordered supplies to be sent to him there from Lynchburg.

Lee's forces were increasingly exhausted. Overnight, he led his men on a quick march west to Rice's Station on the Southside Railroad. On the way, he lost large numbers of sick and starving soldiers, who gave up the march through sheer exhaustion.

LEE SURRENDERS

At 1:00 P.M. on April 9—Palm Sunday—Lee rode to Appomattox Court House. There he signed the surrender of the first great army of the Confederacy to Ulysses S. Grant in the parlor of Wilbur McLean's house, marking the start of the end of the Civil War.

Battle of Sayler's Creek

Union forces were closing in on Lee's flank and rear. On April 6 the pursuers caught up with the rear of the Confederate army near Sayler's Creek. During the fighting that followed, a small Union force of about 600 infantry and cavalry set out to destroy High Bridge to prevent Lee crossing the Appomattox River. Instead, the unit became cut off. Deciding to sacrifice the command in order to delay Lee's march, its officers charged

1864–1865
December–January

CIVIL WAR

DECEMBER 13, GEORGIA
Union troops capture Fort McAllister near Savannah.

DECEMBER 15, TENNESSEE
At the Battle of Nashville, the Confederate Army of Tennessee is defeated by the Union Army of the Cumberland.

DECEMBER 20, GEORGIA
The Confederate garrison escapes from Savannah.

DECEMBER 21, GEORGIA
Sherman and his men enter Savannah unopposed at the conclusion of the March to the Sea.

OTHER EVENTS

DECEMBER 8, VATICAN Pope Pius IX publishes the Syllabus of Errors, which condemns liberalism and reformism.

December

the advancing Confederate columns. Both commanders and many of their men were killed in the attempt.

The fighting at Sayler's Creek cost Lee about one-third of the men who had set out from Amelia Court House. Between 7,000 and 8,000 of his army were killed, wounded, or captured in the action, including six generals.

Final moves

On April 7, Lee led his exhausted men over the Appomattox River. He headed for Lynchburg, with the Union troops in pursuit. Confederate supplies had reached Appomattox Station, but they were captured by Sheridan's cavalry. Lee sent 1,600 infantry and 2,400 cavalry to fight Sheridan, but with little success.

The ruins of the Richmond arsenal in April 1865. As they fled, Confederates reduced much of the city to rubble.

Lee was trapped between Union forces. Some of his junior officers suggested that he should scatter his army so they could fight on using guerrilla warfare. But it was clear to Lee that even if 10,000 of his 15,000 troops escaped—which was unlikely—they were not enough to wage an effective campaign. He had run out of options. Lee declared: "There is nothing left for me to do but to go and see General Grant, and I would rather die a thousand deaths."

LINCOLN ASSASSINATED

On the evening of April 14, 1865, shortly after the end of the war, President Lincoln and his wife were at Ford's Theater in Washington, D.C. As the audience laughed during a performance of the popular comedy *Our American Cousin*, the actor John Wilkes Booth shot Lincoln in the back of the head before fleeing the theater. Booth shouted "Sic semper tyrannis! (So it always is with tyrants) The South is avenged!" The president was carried to a boarding house across the street. Despite the best efforts of the doctors who attended the president, Lincoln had been mortally wounded. He died shortly before 7.30 A.M. the following day.

JANUARY 15, NORTH CAROLINA
Wilmington, the last port in Confederate hands, is closed.

JANUARY 19, SOUTH CAROLINA
General Sherman vows to march through the Carolinas.

JANUARY 31, VIRGINIA
Robert E. Lee is named general-in-chief of all the Confederate armies.

JANUARY 4, UNITED STATES
The New York Stock Exchange opens its first permanent headquarters.

JANUARY 27, PERU
Peru's independence is established in a treaty with Spain.

JANUARY 31, UNITED STATES The House of Representatives approves an amendment to the Constitution abolishing slavery; it will become the Thirteenth Amendment.

Surrender of the Confederacy

Although the South was clearly defeated, the process of ending the Civil War took several weeks after General Robert E. Lee surrendered on April 9, 1865.

President Jefferson Davis and his cabinet flee after Richmond falls to the Union.

Lee was the general-in-chief of all the Confederate armies fighting in the war. He had surrendered to Ulysses S. Grant, who had similar authority over all the Union armies. But neither man was able to conclude a nationwide peace that would

1865
February–March

CIVIL WAR

FEBRUARY 3, VIRGINIA
President Lincoln and Confederate representatives fail to agree a diplomatic ending to the war.

FEBRUARY 16, SOUTH CAROLINA
Columbia surrenders to General Sherman's Union troops.

FEBRUARY 17, SOUTH CAROLINA
As Union troops enter Columbia, someone sets fire to cotton bales. Over half of the city is destroyed in a huge blaze.

FEBRUARY 27, KENTUCKY
Confederate guerrilla leader William C. Quantrill and his band attack civilians in Hickman.

OTHER EVENTS

FEBRUARY 12, UNITED STATES
Henry Highland Garnet becomes the first African American to speak in the House of Representatives.

FEBRUARY 22, UNITED STATES
Tennessee adopts a new state constitution that outlaws slavery.

February

end the war. Early in 1865 President Abraham Lincoln had told Grant that national peace was a political rather than a military question. It had to be resolved between the U.S. government and the seceded states, not between generals. When Grant met Lee at Appomattox Court House, their discussions only dealt with the surrender of Lee's Army of Northern Virginia.

Lincoln had decided that peace would only come when each of the seceded states returned to the Union. The returning states also had to accept the new terms of the Constitution. They included the Thirteenth Amendment of January 1865, which abolished slavery. But the end of the war also clearly depended on the surrender of all the Confederate armies.

Joseph E. Johnston (right) surrenders to William T. Sherman (left) on April 26.

A series of surrenders

The surrender of the Army of Northern Virginia was a subdued occasion, even among the victorious Northern army. The soldiers on both sides were exhausted. Grant set the tone of mutual respect when he ordered his men to stop a 100-gun salute that someone had organized to celebrate victory. The whole process took three days.

There were still three major Confederate forces left in the field. The most important was the army of General Joseph E.

MARCH 2, VIRGINIA
The Shenandoah Valley is in Union control after the Confederates lose the Battle of Waynesboro.

MARCH 3, WASHINGTON, D.C.
The U.S. Congress sets up the Freedmen's Bureau to help deal with the problems resulting from the sudden freeing of tens of thousands of slaves.

MARCH 13, RICHMOND
The Confederate Congress passes a law authorizing the use of black troops.

MARCH 19, NORTH CAROLINA
Joseph E. Johnston attempts to stop the march of Union general William T. Sherman through the Carolinas in the Battle of Bentonville; he is defeated late the following day.

MARCH 4, UNITED STATES
Abraham Lincoln is inaugurated for his second term as president.

MARCH 18, SOUTH AMERICA
Paraguay goes to war with the Triple Alliance of Brazil, Argentina, and Uruguay.

George A. Custer (bottom left) awaits a Confederate flag of truce on April 9.

Johnston, facing William T. Sherman in North Carolina. The others were the armies of Richard Taylor in eastern Louisiana, Alabama, and Mississippi; and Edmund Kirby Smith's Army of the Trans-Mississippi, west of the Mississippi River.

In talks on April 17 and 18, Johnston and Sherman agreed to a surrender. By now, the Union had a new president after the assassination of Abraham Lincoln, who died on April 15. President Andrew Johnson refused to approve the surrender, as its terms covered political as well as military matters. He sent Grant to North Carolina to order Sherman to renegotiate in line with the terms agreed upon at Appomattox. On April 26 Johnston signed a new surrender that dealt strictly with military matters. His men were to surrender their arms and return home. No action would be taken against them by the United States.

By this time Richard Taylor was discussing terms with Union General Edward R.S. Canby. In the West, Union General John Pope in New Orleans had written to Kirby Smith encouraging him to surrender. But Kirby Smith was under pressure to fight on. In military terms, further resistance was useless, but there were still some politicians and junior officers who hoped to continue the war in the West. They included Confederate governors from Arkansas, Louisiana, and

A UNION HERO

The brilliant young Union General George A. Custer (1839–1876) accepted the first Confederate flag of truce in April 1865. He also attended Lee's surrender at Appomattox Court House. But he is best known for the Battle of Little Bighorn of 1876, when he and all 231 of his men died fighting the Sioux and Cheyenne in Montana.

1865
April–May

CIVIL WAR

APRIL 1, VIRGINIA
The Battle of Five Forks ends in defeat for the Confederate Army of Northern Virginia.

APRIL 2, VIRGINIA
Grant attacks Petersburg and the Confederates start a retreat from Petersburg and Richmond.

APRIL 6, VIRGINIA
Lee loses 8,000 men to Union attacks at the Battle of Sayler's Creek.

APRIL 7, VIRGINIA
Grant asks Lee for his army's surrender; Lee asks for terms.

APRIL 9, VIRGINIA
Lee surrenders to Ulysses S. Grant at Appomattox Courthouse.

OTHER EVENTS

April

Missouri, as well as a subordinate officer, General "Jo" Shelby. Confederate President Jefferson Davis, meanwhile, had fled with the rest of his government into Georgia. He hoped to cross the Mississippi River and continue the war in the West.

Final surrender

Despite such unrealistic hopes, most of the remnants of the Confederacy finally gave up in May. Canby took Taylor's surrender in Alabama, and on May 10 Jefferson Davis was captured by Union cavalry in Georgia. On June 2 Kirby Smith surrendered at Galveston, Texas. On June 23, in Indian Territory, Stand Watie became the last Confederate general to surrender his command.

Even now, some diehard Confederates refused to accept surrender. They included Jo Shelby, who took 600 men with him into Mexico to try to find a way to continue the struggle.

On June 6 Confederate prisoners of war who took an oath of allegiance to the United States began to be released. On June 10 President Johnson appointed new governors for the former Confederate states. But it was not until August 20, 1866, that Johnson officially declared the Civil War over, proclaiming that "The insurrection is at an end."

In this etching of 1866, a wounded soldier is happily welcomed home after the Civil War.

CEREMONY OF SURRENDER

After Lee's surrender at Appomattox there seemed to be a sense of loss among many Union soldiers. This feeling was evident on April 12, when the Army of Northern Virginia marched out for the last time to lay down its arms and battle flags at a ceremony of formal surrender.

As the Confederates came down the Union lines, bugles ordered the men in blue to "carry arms," a salute to their enemy that the Southerners gallantly responded to in kind: "honor answering honor," in the words of Union General Joshua L. Chamberlain. It was a worthy end to the hard-fought war in Virginia.

APRIL 14, WASHINGTON, D.C.
President Lincoln is shot while watching a play at the theater.

APRIL 15, WASHINGTON, D.C.
Lincoln dies from his injuries; Vice-President Andrew Johnson becomes president.

APRIL 26, NORTH CAROLINA
Confederate General Joseph E. Johnston surrenders to General William T. Sherman.

MAY 10, GEORGIA
Confederate President Jefferson Davis is captured and taken into custody.

MAY 29, WASHINGTON, D.C.
President Andrew Johnson grants an amnesty and pardon to Confederate soldiers who will take an oath of allegiance to the Constitution.

APRIL 21, UNITED STATES
Lincoln's funeral train leaves Washington, D.C.; Lincoln's body is carried in a Pullman sleeping car.

APRIL 27, UNITED STATES 2,000 Union soldiers aboard the riverboat *Sultana* die when it catches fire and sinks on the Mississippi River in Tennessee.

MAY 1, UNITED STATES
Walt Whitman publishes "Drum Taps," his long poem about the Civil War.

NEED TO KNOW

Some of the subjects covered in this book feature in many state curricula. These are topics you should understand.

People:
Abraham Lincoln
Robert E. Lee
Ulysses S. Grant
William T. Sherman

Strategy:
Union blockade
March to the Sea
Siege warfare
Cutting communications

Politics:
Lincoln's reelection
Hardship in the South
North's economic strength
Black Americans

KNOW THIS

This section summarizes two major themes of this book: the political dominance of the North and the strategies of both sides.

POLITICS

MISSISSIPPI RIVER
Since the capture of Vicksburg in July 1863, the Union had controlled the Mississippi River; the Confederacy was split in two, with the eastern part unable to receive supplies from the West.

BLACK SOLDIERS
The Union was quick to recruit African American soldiers, despite the reluctance of some commanding officers. This gave it a large supply of manpower compared to the South, which did not recruit black soldiers until March 1865, when it was too late.

RESOURCES
The Union blockade had effectively halted Southern imports, and upheaval caused by the war had greatly cut farm production and the amount of food available. While life in the North carried on largely as normal, in the South people were close to despair.

RECONSTRUCTION
In his second inaugural speech, President Lincoln promised that reconstruction would take place "with malice toward none." But in order to achieve the peace, Lincoln and his generals waged highly destructive war and insisted that the Confederate surrender was unconditional.

STRATEGY

- The North tried to sever the two halves of the Confederacy by capturing the whole of the Mississippi River and besieging the town that held them together, Vicksburg.
- Union general William T. Sherman marched through Georgia and the Carolinas, causing great damage; his aim was to convince civilians to stop supporting the war.
- Sherman captured coastal ports; this tightened the Union blockade and also allowed the Union to supply forces in the Deep South by sea.
- Ulysses S. Grant led an overland campaign toward Richmond, Virginia, forcing Robert E. Lee to defend the Confederate capital.
- The only hope for the South was to combine its armies, but Grant made sure that was impossible.
- Grant achieved final victory by cutting Lee off from his lines of supply.

TEST YOURSELF

These questions will help you discover what you have learned from this book.
Check the pages listed in the answers below.

1. **What river defended Richmond, Virginia, from the Union army?**

2. **Why did General Grant regret his final charge at the Battle of Cold Harbor?**

3. **What defeat made General Sherman turn to a strategy of maneuver?**

4. **Why was General Hardee surprised at the Battle of Jonesboro?**

5. **How did the fall of Atlanta help President Abraham Lincoln?**

6. **What was Admiral David Farragut's famous order at Mobile Bay?**

7. **Why did General Lee abandon Petersburg?**

8. **What was the name for the strategy behind Sherman's "March to the Sea"?**

9. **After which defeat did General John Bell Hood resign?**

10. **Why did General George E. Pickett miss the Battle of Five Forks?**

ANSWERS

1. Chickahominy River (see page 13). 2. Because he lost many casualties for no gain (see page 15). 3. Kennesaw Mountain (see page 17). 4. He blundered into the whole Union army (see page 19). 5. It was a major reason he was reelected as president in November 1864 (see page 23). 6. "Damn the torpedoes! Full speed ahead!" (see page 25). 7. His supply lines were threatened (see page 27). 8. "Total war" (see page 29). 9. Battle of Nashville (see page 35). 10. He was having a picnic (see page 35).

GLOSSARY

artillery Heavy guns such as cannons that fire shells and balls a long way

batteries Groups of heavy guns, such as cannons

bayonet A sharp dagger that is attached to the end of a rifle for hand-to-hand fighting

blockade Measures aimed at preventing trade by using ships to intercept vessels heading toward port

bombardment A period of artillery fire aimed at a particular target

brigade A military unit made up of about 5,000 soldiers divided into two to six regiments

cavalry Soldiers that fight on horseback

counterattack An attack launched on the enemy after it has already attacked

division The largest unit of an army: it is made up of three or four brigades

entrench To dig in to a defensive position

flank The side of a military unit or line

fortifications Positions that are protected by strong defenses such as trenches or walls

garrison A group of soldiers who occupy a military post

infantry Soldiers who fight on foot

ironclad A ship that is protected by a covering of iron armor

militia Part of a country's army made up of citizens who are called on to serve in times of emergency

regiment A military unit; at full strength, a regiment had 10 companies of 100 men

rout A total defeat

siege A military attack in which an army or city is surrounded and cut off in order to force its surrender.

skirmish A minor fight between enemy forces

strategic Something that is important to an overall plan, even if it is not very important on its own

FURTHER READING

BOOKS

Abnett, Dan. *The Battle of the Wilderness: Deadly Inferno* (Graphic Battles of the Civil War). Rosen Publishing Group, 2007.

Berry, Carrie. *A Confederate Girl: The Diary of Carrie Berry, 1864* (Diaries, Letters, and Memoirs). Blue Earth Books, 2000.

Bircher, William. *A Civil War Drummer Boy: the Diary of William Bircher, 1861–1865* (Diaries, Letters, and Memoirs). Blue Earth Books, 2000.

Bobrick, Benson. *The Battle of Nashville: George H. Thomas and the Most Decisive Battle of the Civil War*. Knopf Books for Young Readers, 2010.

Cohn, Scotti. *Beyond Their Years: Stories of Sixteen Civil War Children*. TwoDot, 2003.

Editors of Time for Kids. *Clara Barton: Angel of the Battlefield* (Time for Kids Biographies). Collins, 2008.

Haislip, Phyllis Hall. *Anybody's Hero: The Battle of Old Men and Young Boys*. White Mane Kids, 2003.

Jerome, Kate Boehm. *Civil War Sub: the Mystery of the* Hunley. Grosset & Dunlop, 2002.

King, David C. *Civil War and Reconstruction*. (American Heritage, American Voices). Wiley, 2003.

Olson, Kay Melchisedech. *The Assassination of Abraham Lincoln*. (Graphic Library). Capstone Press, 2005.

Stanchak, John E. *Eyewitness Civil War*. Dorling Kindersley, 2000.

Swanson, James L. *Chasing Lincoln's Killer*. Scholastic Press, 2009.

WEBSITES

www.civilwar.com
Comprehensive privately run, moderated site on the Civil War

www.civil-war.net
Collection of images, written sources, and other material about the Civil War

www.historyplace.com/civilwar
The History Place Civil War timeline

www.pbs.org/civilwar
PBS site supporting the Ken Burns film *The Civil War*

www.civilwar.si.edu
The Smithsonian Institution's Civil War collections, with essays, images, and other primary sources

INDEX